D0268145

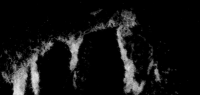

SONIC WHITE POISE

First published in 2021 by
The Dedalus Press
13 Moyclare Road
Baldoyle
Dublin D13 K1C2
Ireland

www.dedaluspress.com

ISBN 978-1-910251-84-3 (paperback)
ISBN 978-1-910251-85-0 (hardback)

Dedalus Press titles are available in Ireland
from Argosy Books (www.argosybooks.ie) and in the UK
from Inpress Books (www.inpressbooks.co.uk).

Cover image: *Assemblage No 4* by Patrick Cotter.

The Dedalus Press receives financial assistance from
The Arts Council / An Chomhairle Ealaíon.

SONIC WHITE POISE

PATRICK COTTER

DEDALUS PRESS

ACKNOWLEDGEMENTS

Gratitude to the editors of the following publications where a number of these poems, or earlier versions of them, previously appeared:

In Ireland: *The Honest Ulsterman. The Irish Times, The Penny Dreadful, Poetry Ireland Review* and *The Stinging Fly.*
In Britain: *Declaimer, The Financial Times, Five Dials, London Review of Books, The Morning Star, PN Review, Poetry Review, Poetry Wales* and *The Rialto.*
In North America: *All Hollow, The Ambush Review, The Awl, The Cortland Review, Pilgrimage Review, Poetry, Poetry Congeries* and *Riddle Fence.*
Elsewhere: *Live Encounters* and *Pratik.*

And in the following anthologies:

Jeune Poésie d'Irlande, editors Paul Bensimon & Clíona Ní Ríordain (Editions Illador, Paris 2015); *11 Irish Poets,* editor Julijana Velikovska (PNV, Skopje 2016); *On the Banks, Cork City in Poems and Songs,* editor Allannah Hopkin (The Collins Press, Cork, 2016) and *Cork Words,* editor Patricia Looney (Cork City Libraries, 2020).

'Madra' received the 2013 Keats Shelley Poetry Prize.
'The Discoveries of Thomas Fynch' was runner-up for the inaugural Dermot Healy Poetry Prize.
'Mais Feliz' took second prize in the 2013 Bailieborough Poetry Competition.
'Song of a Maid' was highly commended in the 2015 Manchester Cathedral Poetry Competition.

Contents

Side A

War Songs in a Time of Peace

Bestiary

The Lee Road Codex

For my parents, Tom & Mary

Side A

Wounded Enough

The sculptor sits with his head in his hands,
waiting for the committee to stop deliberating
as they bicker within earshot of his angel statue
white marble luminous in the midday sun.
Should its eyes be blindfolded? A spear through
its ribs? Would it be better with shattered wings?
The days of triumphalism are ended, belonging only
to history books. Everything must now display
its wounds to reflect the vulnerable world.
On and on they argue. *What is wounded enough?*
How much is hyperbole? The sculptor shapes in his mind
an angel of yore, wings outspread, devoid
of the sunglasses of irony, the sneakers of modernity,
ready to soar away from all of this.

Music for Ghosts

As an offering to the ghosts
I left some music playing
when I shut the door

on the empty house.
Even when a house is full
of ghosts we say it's empty,

empty when you step out
and there's no one left inside
breathing. 'Lost in Music' by Sister

Sledge and 'Good Times' by Chic
both by the same composer.
You might say if I was truly

considerate of ghosts I would pick
songs more than forty years old.
I should leave playing tunes

by Cole Porter or the sort warbled
by Count John McCormack.
But I believe leaving ghosts

any music in an empty house
all to themselves while the dial
of the electric meter spins

is a gift and not only the living,
but ghosts too deserve harmony.
Even when a house has every wall

lined with books we can call it empty;
even when plants exhale from inside
every window we can call it empty;

when I am sitting on the stairs staring
at the shadows thrown by the morning sun,
as you sleep under stars in a distant timezone

Oisín

With a dead tongue I named you
'little deer'. You had tossed under
your mother's skin, pushing shapes

like shrunken antlers behind a satin veil.
Somehow I saw it all leading to this:
the struggles with your mother

the scripted tears and slammed doors
the walkings-out and walkings-in
the candles lit and the prayers begun;

all to your father to be the first to hold you.
My green surgical gown, disposable
skullcap like some priestly garb

or butcher's apparel. You taking
the world in with a yawn, blood-stained
forehead and eyes blurred as if staring

through a dozen bottles thick with vodka.
The surgeon put a needle to your mother's belly.
Her trolley shin-high in a swill of blood

and amniotic liquor. I cried God's name
silent, inside my skull. Chaffinch song
bickered through the open window like a chorus.

Mais Feliz

For penance he glued sandpaper to the piano keys
– red on the ivory, yellow on the ebony, and played
what had been their song, a slow Brazilian ballad
sweet in its melancholy. He started by pressing
lightly (though the keys still scorched his fingertips)
gradually speeding the tempo until he finished
the piece in some Rachmaninov frenzy.
He winced and groaned, yelped and cried
with each note, making all the noises she complained
he never did with her, between the sheets.
He placed the home-made card
saying *sorry* and the digital recording
of his remorse in a manila envelope
stamped with whorlless crimson fingerprints.

Portrait of a Town in Economic Distress

Recall the derelict canning-plant where
we embraced; its hint of stark sardine
– a half remembered scent too faint for the nose

more like an olfactory ghost haunting.
I was distracted by the iron light-fitting
without a bulb whining in the wind rushing

through the glassless window, the light-fitting's edges
rusted to the same hue as your spare, wispy,
dry-as-a-leaf pubes; my thoughts loose as I lay

beneath your proliferating orgasms;
my ass the medium by which you kneaded
the disturbed floor dust. I was detached as if

a mere witness to the unwilled act
of the long braided rope of your hair prodding
my chest with each coital swoop; the russet hair

which was the provocateur of anxiety
in the dreams of all the boys of the town who
could never speak to you as you strolled the streets

with an armadillo on a leash, your hair
crowned with a tiara of writhing, starving
iguanas: greenness being brought to market.

Dinka

Beware, Malagasy girl. There's too much white in me
to make a Dinka, even with you. See this one:

an obelisk of a man. Five boys with coltish limbs
could climb and cling from him as from a tree.

His skin black as this coiling eel in my ceramic sink; the map
of his body a riposte to a white supremacist's delusional dream.

His rested cock pendulous and heavy as an iron chisel.
His tongue a skinned strawberry glistening on coal.

Place him in a Venetian square – watch him
negotiate the empty space as if still weaving a way

between the scimitars of his cattle's white horns;
the cattle yet yielding milk from the dry season's ashy earth.

The cattle of a Nubian *Táin* whose horned heroic head
sits on the shoulders of a pharaonic god, minion

and messenger of Amun. Dinka – giant man
so short in years none grow slack or grey:

sculpture of flesh perfect unto death. Choose me
and you will have white, white hair; a man

of uncooked dough to love you to the grave
white as the bones inside of me, the bones

you would dig up, dress in the reddest silk
so I would be benevolent after death

to our sons, who could not be Dinka.

Sleeptalker In A Cold Climate

pour MJD

Over the crimson path of your tongue
my thrusts oust a friendly fiendkin:
a sprite spitting idioms of joyful protest

– plosive French whispers rustling
midst wreathing limbs; you're a sleeptalker
I dare not rouse from your oblivious lair.

In flaccid aftermath, you fail to recall
any of the ghostly gabble. Your body's
jet, my flint, lie in a florid zebra weave.

When you stir to leave, the stars
flicker in weakness. Your quitting
back reflects the lunar sheen.

Morning, blanketed by your scent
shedding covers is like stripping skin.
Diving upright into cold is keen pain

as is fleeing the gazelle's form you impressed
in my bed. Hell is the absence of your heat
on my arms. Hellish the ghostly chill.

Occidental Perspective

I swipe your eyebrow and listen for the thrum of vanilla's
faintest essence. Your voice's humming back-tones hang
in the air, piquant as falling sheaves, separated sheaf
by sheaf by random scents, by waves of eye-gaze gamma.
Not long ago, with your body, you declared your broad-front
offensive on all my senses. I scrape my ear over
the gosling-bumps of your back, rake the music
of sallow, plucked from my own strung longish lobes
as with the aye-aye's lorish folk fingers you've feared
in all your sleep-sojourns, since a childhood spent among
the baobabs' fortress boles, their Onive-washed roots.
Though you have never thought it, there are those
who would say the forest's charring scorch, encroaching
from the edges, is the otherness of my pale – from near the Pole –
    touch.

Anthracite Love

How blond still the young coal miner's hair.
Of his skin, only his lips and nipples resist the dust.
His lover is thrilled to see him thus while youth
still shapes the contours of his arms. The fine grit
transfers between them when they touch. He loves marking

the whiteness of her skin, she loves the streaks
where she has ground him clean. As a boy he played
at being preacher; lecturing stones and fallen leaves
as his peers tusselled around him. Of women
he was more used to seeing their backs, kneeling in church.

Now he mumbles prayers in her armpits, vespers
to the down of her aureoles. She reflects one can tongue
only so much of culm. She would like him to make toys.
A man who sells dolls could never dig underground.
After her first baby she will have eaten enough of coal.

Ghost Fest

The ghosts of this house have taken to mocking my grief.
Even my faux-fleece eyemask fails to fence them out,
the ghosts of this house, house of shudders and creaks.
They prise aside my eyelids as I sleep, and bounce

on my corneas with ectoplasmic luminance.
Impatient to waken me and engage them in 'fun',
the ghosts of this house have taken to strewing
glass shards beneath my naked feet – from gin tumblers

tottering into flamboyant leaps off bookshelves
to tea-light jars exploding suddenly after a flame's
snuffing. Some kinds of glass are safe from their sabotage:
the new triple-glazed frames I had installed last winter

and the stained glass crafted by my Icelandic ex-lover.
He of the now tundric froideur. The ghosts of this house
cannot spook their way through stone too thick or through argon
or through the leaded frames and pot-metal panes of stained glass.

They have been trapped in the house for weeks, goading me
to unlock my front door. The Barrack Street Festival of Ghosts
happens soon and my house-sharing spectres like to rehearse
with their motley mates from mixed centuries in the open air;

marching to venerable tuneage by generations of dead members
of the Barrack Street Brass Band; to *God Save the Queen* from
the abstemious 1837 iteration or to *Lipizzaners Prancing*
from the Beamish-guzzling 1913 lot. Anyway, my boy from Fluðir,

he of the kumquat-shaped, boysenberry eyes had enough
of rowdy revenants: *Even Erik the Red wouldn't stomach lodging*
with this malevolent Casperish ménage, he whined in his
scandalised Scandi intonations. His snow nipples never melted

on the tongue but hardened to moist flickable stone.
Stones I'll never fling again as the ghosts of this house suck
up my tears and spit them back at me, like weird indoor weather.
Oh, I'll make sure they'll miss this year the non-improvised groans

and gurgling of Dan the Black and Tan, half his hairy skull
flapping over his ear onto his shoulder after a run-in
with the teenage Mick Finn and his polished Mauser, and Mick Finn
himself, raw-necked from the rope which wrangled him.

They'll forego the joys of the 18th century camp followers of Blue
    Coat Lane
shrieking as they pass the Cameroonian coiffeur
(where local white girls used to reap their cornrow extensions)
all because these mangy sprites mock my grief over him named Leif.

Face

Tassajara, Zen Monastery, Springs Resort California

It was sunrise at Tassajara when I came
across a novice monk with legs crossed and eyes closed
in meditation while morning's soft Lalique light

sought out the last clumps of darkness lurking under
bushes and behind the low stone wall. Mist, exhaling
from the close-by stream, moistened the dry mountain air

and soft water-mantras were uttered by the tongue
of the stream as it rolled over the smoothened stones
within. No shapeless robes could hide her body and

at first I thought of moving on, so I could be
one fewer worldly distraction as she sat so
like a saint, so detached from the well-honed contours

of her well-formed face, her shorn, bowed, head.
But the mystic archer let fly a shot, pierced
me with his karmic providence. The stepped-upon

cinder path played percussion beneath my feet. I
became bold in my stares and my glances licked her
body like dragon flame. Was it pride or nonchalance

or the stern command of a shuso which had her
squatting here all alone, prominent, on display,
in all her Buddhist chic, here by the hot badlands

of the weekender tourist trail, between cabins
and sulphurous springs, where wretched such as I passed
frequently, sometimes open to redemption but

more often, mindful of the materialist charms
of the bulgar pilaffs and jicama salads,
the hot plunges and hike trails through the wilderness?

Bronze bells tolled in answer but made no difference.

Prayer Service

for Nuala Ní Dhomhnaill

Mid-morning. And the late November sun had finally leapt
over the hurdle of our high, green latitude – cloudless, bright,
casting sharp shadows. I was carried along on the racing train;

watched fields pass by like fleeting strangers. A paddock
was streaked by chopped trees, laid out like helpless bodies
in triage. Finches hopped branch to quivering branch,

perplexed the old rowans formed no longer the hedgerow
generations fledged in. At Heuston Station the chef
of the Galway Hooker spooned champignons, white pudding,

ham, onto my wide-brimmed plate before I left for the mosque,
wondering, without worrying too much, whether molecules
of *banbh* on my breath would affront Allah. But wondering

was as dandelion seed in a storm when the men knelt down
to chant, with even the smallest boy fully devoted.
I felt the force of their prayer shudder through me from bone

to sinew; the gleaming coffin of wood as beautiful
as once the freshly-washed body sealed inside, the body
of the man I had never met but knew you loved, who had

loved you, praying now above me in the high gallery
with all the other scarf-covered women like some old scene:
an Irish church you and your beloved were banished from.

Ghost Dogs

for Isso

Ghost dogs are tethered to a world
they cannot smell and loll
in acceptance, soft chins resting
between splayed paws. Their faint
spectral shimmers barely visible
to one another and not at all
to the living. Our world of sight
and sound is for them a dull world
of curt limitations, a vast, barren
plain of olfactory ennui;
all the earth's smells sealed behind
caulked invisible seams.
Even their own ectoplasm
reeks of nothing
and there is nowhere to skitter
with nose skimming the ground
as the breeze purfles the topmost bristles
of a raised curious tail. All of this
they miss with an acceptance
I'm developing as my hair greys
sitting in a municipal park
the sun's oblique rays gilding
the silky, reflective, fragrant tresses
of even the most raven-haired beauties
to whom I am as invisible as a ghost.

War Songs
in a Time of Peace

Song of a Maid

Aged eight it came to me in a dream
I had been Joan of Arc in a previous life
and at twelve a tarot reader off Charing
Cross Road, with lightning and rain

smiting the pavement, confirmed it.
My spread was a fascia of swords and staves
and all the war-making cards with faces.
God appears to have forsaken me in this life:

I cannot ride a horse or speak French.
The closest I ever get to wearing armour
is my corduroy duffle coat donned on a turbulent day.
I visited an earl's great country house so

I could touch his ancestor's steel breastplates.
When nobody was looking I left the smears
of my fingers and palms. Babysitting
is the highest service I have risen to.

Now fourteen years old, I feel time running
away like a spoilt dog. One child I mind
Oliver, has curls and luminous eyes
of lapis lazuli lifted from a Medici tempera.

His nappies reek of myrrh and frankincense.
And with a shirred gaze he stares often
beyond my shoulder in awe. If I could turn
fast as light, I know I would see the Virgin

waiting for the moment to speak, to intone
on the will of her Son; on what I should say
when I call on the Queen or summon
David Cameron or when François Hollande

seeks out my counsel. Then I will need no horses.
A helicopter gunship will be my chariot
and I will venture forth to dispense
God's indubitable works.

Votive Soldiers

"Be your own bedroom general: there is no braver man than a soldier in the form of a figurine."
—*Airfix Magazine 1961*

Behold this box of jumbled varicoloured lives
I once held daily office with; each a repository
for an imagined soul I would heap into piles
of the damned and the saved. I watched them

suffer many deaths, many resurrections.
Not all were assigned the daydreamt saga
of a hero, or made the renowned shaper
of a bedroom history; but this one of the Afrika Korps,

field glasses permanently to his face, liberated the second
floor landing, opposite the bathroom, several times
from grey-hued Soviet occupation. And this red
Roman legionnaire with flaked paint, cracked base,

truncated gladius, become emperor, promoted
through the ranks after a humble beginning
at a convent school bazaar, peddled by the nuns
like common pillaged booty, bought for a bright

new decimal penny. And this *British* officer, Webley
at the ready, running for his life, is really West Waterford gentry.
They suffered actual attritions too: vanished by the platoon
into the acquisitive pockets of the boys from the police barracks

or swept by the battalion by my mother into the ashbin's abyss,
a kinetic cleansing when their billeting on her linoleum floors
had stretched too long beyond teatime. After forty years I recall
their stories still, more clearly than many of my own.

I can remember each of their frozen poses and playwear scars, their stoicism as something truly holy, not plastic, not leaden.

Viewing Bill Brandt's *East End Girl Dances the Lambeth Walk 1939* in 2015

Pudding-bowl hairlines, trousers and dresses
grey and pink, rumpled as the lettuce they never get to eat
the children act like refugees expelled from boom time

to a dystopian past without socialist victories
or unions trading in strength; none of them tall enough
to earn hand-me-down-the-moon as a legendary nickname.

Their haircuts, their clothes are the best this past can give
and yet they laugh, punching one another on the chests
as the oldest struts with brazen action and a smirk

she's swiped from the faces of women her mother
maligns as 'slatterns' who stumble from *the Crown
and Unicorn* late on a Saturday night, each ready

to swing lockfisted from another's course tresses.
Pavement is the children's gallery, chalk the medium
for all the art in their lives. Their only audience

an old man and an old dog who have seen it all too often
to clap, yap or yawn. Over the smoky roofs, against
the dustbin sky, looms the sharp silhouette

of the largest ship on the docks, Hamburg owned,
disgorging more children with stones and gold
and rosy mountains to their names, just in time to greet

the fin-tailed bombs that will hurl down
whistling like grim wolves.

Dog Morse

The dog down my street knows Morse I swear,
his pitch, his expression as rare as Stan Getz.
I know him by his barks alone.

With a swaggering tail he could pass me in the street
or piddle on my boots and I would not know him.
I've noted his messages down

but the language he speaks remains a mystery at times
just last night he signalled the words:
"Jxtugh nwxrut hejwrt mnpw"

You might laugh, but last week he barked in English:

"The yellow bittern's song
Enters the dark quadrant
When it is hungry
The yellow dog's whine
Happens some days
To hit the same notes
As the song of the yellow bittern."

It's possible he is a spy or the instrument of a spy.
Who knows? Maybe the dog is not the author of his own words
but prodded into barking in Morse.

Sometimes he barks and barks and never receives a reply.
Perhaps I should be analysing the noise road traffic makes
or the staccato of raindrops. If there are rules to this game

I don't know what they are.
Who says you can't message in dog barks
and respond by raindrops?

Before The Revolution

after Frank Espada, for Martín Espada

Before the revolution one must have time to curl one's hair
to roll it in cylinders of prickly plastic and wait as it dries
while hanging out a window, listening to the disciple of Lenin
have his say, purling his lips around the mic, loving it as Elvis
would, not like some standoffish white boy with a trust fund.

Before the revolution time to play guitar in the park;
your friend strumming along on the mouth harp; your woman
nowhere within earshot anyway, but you sing that song
of her spurning departure, telenovella-like in complexity.
Before the revolution, time to sell the screenrights
to your melodic melancholy.

Before the revolution, before your tenth birthday
time to jack a car or at least rip out the distributor cap
from the fool who left the white sedan outside your door
like godmother's morphed pumpkin, an albino hearse
its hood begging to be popped like a ripened pod
to reap the metal seed of the mechanic's workshop.

Before the revolution time to photograph
the neighbourhood's kids, hair jungle-wild
face unirrigated, clothes unpressed like rippling rivers.

Before the revolution time for Malcolm
to shoot himself under the chin
with a loaded finger.

Before the revolution time to ....
Before the revolution ....
Before ....
Be ....

By A Ruin Near Drogheda

That midsummer night during the moonlit hooley
he spurned her invite and slumbered instead
inside his father's tomb. Against one wall
a stele with carved recesses, each filled

with a special offering: the blue ribbon
won by his champion landrace;
the mirror used to detect the interred's last breath;
an apple from the tree he had planted as a child;

the Orange Lodge bowler the family
was ashamed of and too afraid to throw away;
the candle, prize of some secret initiation
nobody spoke about and the carcass

of the homing pigeon which had carried
messages from his mistress, who now danced
overhead alone in the crowd, her belly
enwrapped by a big brown belt handed down

the generations, sporting, as the legend goes
Oliver Cromwell's stolen buckle which glowed
hot and red every September eleventh since 1649.

Homecoming

The returned conscript dances with his mother,
unscathed body crowned by his beaming smile;
her yellow-ribboned hair the only bright thing

on her angled, wistful head. He still has all his mother.
She has just one of three sons. She knows it's good
he still has two legs to kick with, two hands to scoop

her into air. Her neighbour's boy's body
ends at his thighs. Strays on the street
snap at his chair's wheels. Yet her silent wish –
to hold three half-sons rather than one whole.

No amount of waltzes or polkas make
her forget her sons in the ground –
if that's where they are; exploded to
shreds, red spray and crow food.

War Games

So rare these days to come across
small boys playing at soldiers;
the mouthed sounds of bullets

in flight; the simulated gargles
of death and the choreographed
leap to the ground as if knocked

by shrapnel or gas. The field I pass
on a Sunday stroll is sprinkled
with little motley corpses. A few blend

with the colours of grass; with most
their blue, purple and teal T-shirts
gleam like wounds in the landscape.

One has brought a sword
to the gunfight, but knowing
the smug old adage he announces

his sword is enchanted.
As to a wingless Saint Michael
the battlefield doffs its dead to him –

who rise with a chuckle
after a light touch of his blade –
the dead felled by plastic

Kalashnikovs whose short
rapid barks ignite the magpies
in their grenade-round cores.

Bestiary

The Hound Artist

The one who clasped the collar on
is as absent as the virtuous family
in the vintage photographs fastened
to the wall behind; as still and dutiful

as the day they lingered for the slow exposure,
as still as this dutiful hound now, not needing
a leash and yet leashed with a long lash of leather
as slack as superfluous. She has a red-

coated, palace guard's inscrutability. One
might think a mouse could skitter across
her paws, a kitten claw at her nose and she
wouldn't flinch. The surrounding room looks

like it would collapse first, the stool with its uneven
legs, the lilting sideboard decades without polish,
the doorway drapes frayed and dustcovered,
the floor unlevel, crying for a screed, and she

too secure and self-assured to even be proud.
Her gaze on me lacks expectation, she appears
as detached as the Buddha, the Buddha in canine
form. I find myself overcome with an unwillingness

to move, not out of fear as before a snarler, a drooler,
a curled-lip fang-revealer, but as before a great artist
who deserves a moment devoid of distraction.
I am in awe of this performance, of an artform

I neither recognise nor understand, perhaps
I am missing the dimension of smell or high decibel
hearing which might explain everything, as I try
to remember how I reached this room, how long ago.

The Shrew

As a small boy I awoke to life's delicacy in small parcels.
I do not speak of miniature men in green and grey, in disarray:
one August morning, sunlight strafed my bunk in a sea-side chalet,
lighting-up casualties from last night's skirmishes – curtain-falls
to my daily Alameins or Waterloos. It had been no less a battle
to stave off sleep, until it struck suddenly like a bullet's hurtle.

Awake after sunrise I stirred and stroked my vellum-
smooth face, pockmarks and bristles were years, flows
of hormones away and as I turned in the twisted bedclothes,
an *Airfix* commando dug into my shoulder as into a glum
shallow foxhole, his arm upstretched, his hand clutching a Mills
grenade – the plastic type, explodable only in the foothills

of a small boy's fantasies. I turned again and my favourite *Timpo*
    knight,
black and errant, slipped through the crack between the narrow bed
and the box-wood wall, into an imagined cold abyss where all
    hope bled.
I slithered to the floor and squeezed beneath, breathless at the sight…
the knight's brave mount had landed on its feet and both horse
    and man
were ready to charge a cowering shrew, pygmy shrew; so short a span

from tail to quivering nose: incredibly small next to the bulk of me.
Loose sand grains all around were swept up in the little flurry
of my exhalation. Soon the only moving thing was the furry
shrew's muzzle. She was so small, like a hairy beetle exuding
    personality.
No sign of a wood louse or ant to snaffle: her being-there was a shock.
I was able to see, as she scuttled away, each one of her whiskers mock.

The Pity of Dogs

Fresh-cut grass is too sweet for the canine nostril,
so while sitting in file as our master commands
we sniff the air for dry turds wafting from a distance
or a whiff of a dead mouse combusting slowly

in the summer heat beyond the line of trees
at the far edge of this field. The alluring mist
of a bitch in heat is probably too much to hope for
but the piquancy of our master's treats

cannot be concealed by the sweatiness of his palms
or the dry musk of his crotch pocket. So we sit
in place, our eagerness urgent, our insides as restless
as our lolling tongues. The pooch next to me sharply

pulls his nose left and up and suddenly I smell it too!
A swallow's dropping in an angled trajectory
heading to the ground, fast, fast, but slower
than its scent-bearing molecules have hit my septum.

Nothing smells new about my master, but one subtle
spice he exudes grows stronger daily, I can smellualize
its black florescence spreading through his lungs.
Each time I lick him now, it is with greater tenderness.

Cowshed

The man who slept in the cowshed leant on the cattle for warmth.
They let him suck milk straight from the teat and he never had a
    hitch
scratching his back on their horns as their bells jangled. If he
    needed

his face scrubbed he would spray himself with grass juice and the
    cows
would lick him clean with their fuzzy tongues. In cafés, people
    shifted
their chairs away from him: he reeked too ripe, like melting
    camembert

or Milleens. One day, in desperate humour, he shrouded his head
in the caul of a just-born calf – it had a lacy-looking quality,
even as it felt tacky as taffy. He heisted the village post office

thinking *nobody will know who I am* – they simply cleared out
his own account and sniggered as he made his get-away.
He owned a perfectly good house, good for living in,

but after his widower dad died he took to the shed.
As a boy he had glimpsed the ghost of a serene, well-limbed
girl milking the cows. So he began to sleep among the mooers

hoping to see her again and after years, when he had forgotten her,
he still slept there. Someday, he mulled, I'll move the cows
into the house, when I have a wife I can share them with.

Lost Tiger

The neighbourhood lost-pet pole, like an emerged
periscope from a subterranean lair of despair

advertising lost cats mostly, dogs too, once
a taciturn budgerigar, once a Russian-grey hamster

but this week a lost tiger, with peregrinating detail
about girth, stripes and a little asymmetrical

white mark, as wispy as cirrus, smack on the nose
as if there was a chance a different lost tiger

roamed the neighbourhood. *Fifi* she answered to,
apparently; could be 'awkward' around Jack Russells

and weighed so much 'can cause damage when playful'.
Occasionally my brain is subsumed by gloom upon seeing

someone has posted a photo of a missing son
who could bloat up later by the harbour's mouth

beneath the bovine moan of the lighthouse, but
always on different, metal, lamp-posts - not the lost-pet pole,

wooden, telegraph, mottled here and there
with preservative tar and the stapled patches

of past posters torn away after a prodigal return
or depleted hope. And now this Panthera satire

a parody of love ruptured, of grief stirred
by absconsion or abduction, traffic mishap.

Maybe it's not a prank, but an intimation of wretchedness
by someone so outcast they never had a pet to lose – so imagined one

and, to sense belonging, posted the loss of their imaginary tiger?
I dialled the number – a real one. It rang and rang and rang.

Portraits of A Single Soul as Different Dogs

My shortest life was as the puppy on a twine leash
pressed close to the face of Kertész's blond boy.
My next life was as the oversized sausage dog
of Wegee's ambivalent non-cis lady.
For Diane Arbus I inhabited a white poodle teacosy
in symmetry with the young lady bartender's platinum beehive.
On the beach in Crete I was the Dalmatian bitch
who could toss her head on cue to Herbert List's
out of frame lisp. Man Ray manically rayographed
me to meld with a cat. Bill Brandt disguised me
as a wagging pebble on a beach beyond
the white expanse of his abstracted lover.
Doisneau pictured me as a wide-eyed innocent
being checked for worms. And later, again,
as one of a pair of shaggy blackhaired rogues
begging in unison on the Rue de la Chapelle,
our tongues hanging out like throbbing palms.
I was the shivering Chihuahua in a glengarry
next to Elliot Erwitt's Great Dane on meaty stilts.
I auditioned for Mapplethorpe but was outshone
by a long-stemmed white orchid and black penis.
Mary Ellen Mark juxtaposed my twelve
distended teats with the full complement
of toes of a Benares beauty.
I am between lives as a rotting mongrel corpse
beneath the floorboards in Ralph Eugene's portrait
of Cranston Ritchie with steel prosthetic claw.
For Dorothea Lange I am the great wooden foxhound
of Troy, Michigan – sandwich boards between my legs,
able to sniff a growing dustbowl states away.
Here I am, nuzzling where I shouldn't
in one of Araki's "lucky holes".

In his first take, John Minihan shot me
in cameo through the transparency
of a yet-to-be princess's sun-soused shift.
For Graciela Iturbide I was a xoloitzcuintle with scalp
tufted like some weird bird, the cloud of crows
overhead wanted so badly to gobble.

Mink

The woman who loved to wear live mink
insisted at first on having their teeth
pulled, but this just led to slobber

all over her lamé Givenchy, so instead
she went with anaesthesia and they curled
her neck with open glistening eyes and teeth

bared as viciously as her own when affronted
by fur objectors. "It's alive!" she'd hiss,
"Leave me alone. Leave one outpost of haut style

survive on this lithe neck." A P.A. followed
with a diamond-studded, patent-leather
crate to put the mink in when everybody,

including the mink, was tired. Once one
revived prematurely over a bowl of Tuscan
hare stew, truffles lending a piquant aroma

to the Prosecco-marinated flesh. With
a graceless drunken lunge it snaffled
the hostess's sapphire-encrusted peacock

brooch right off her breast and was fed
in turn – brooch, fur, teeth and all – to the same
greyhounds which had coursed and killed the hare.

Counterpane

I can't remember when I added the dead mouse
to my collection. Desiccated, flattened, so when
you hold it up by the tail you can twirl it around

like a stiff lollipop. I once thought of framing it
– nothing fancy, one of those €6.99 jobs from Tiger
with a less-is-more, elaboration-free aesthetic going on.

I could imagine the young sales assistant exclaiming
ewww! if she knew what I was buying it for.
Everyone my age while young would have said *yuck*.

What is celebrated by a dead mouse in a frame?
Does it function as a trophy, or memorial
for the tiny soul receptacle radiating warmth

no more, or as some gesture of jejune irony?
Lying now on my new windowsill – the one protected
from the overarching Nile of condensation by the miracle

of double-glazing – it attracts the feagued uninterest
of the neighbour's marmalade tom. Not only his teeth,
but his mind is separated from the answers to those questions,

twice-over.

Peacat

The cat covered in feathers instead of fur
emerged from an egg beneath her mother's teat
betwixt her hairy, mewing siblings. She grew on milk

but earned the love of her family for all their fleas
she swallowed. She was so proud of her bright
varicoloured plumes, she felt complete disdain

for the dull thatch of thrushes and crows. Any strange
moggy who strayed into the neighbourhood and mistook
her curled, heaving, sleeping body for easy fowl

suffered the ignominy of unmerciful scrawls
and the occasional lost eye, as bejewelled as any bright
trifle a magpie would snaffle – and they did, anticipating

with glee the stalking crawl of all feline fools towards
the cat covered in feathers instead of fur. She was as proud
as any cat of her glistening coat, but preened it

like a pigeon rather than with slow grooming licks.
Upon first sight you would expect her to peep
but she mewled and purred like all her foremothers

as, quill by quill, she occasionally moulted
the coat of her mysterious Triassic forefather,
a forgettable fossil, absent forever from her thoughts.

Madra

The dog who read books had nowhere
in his brain for the words to go.

As they streamed in through his eyes, line
by line they re-emerged through each

fibre in his fur with a yelp.
He watched his master's noiseless act

of reading and copied him as
best he could turning the pages

by swishing his nose, swivelling
his head from side to side and top

to bottom over each page. Words
of English left him a shiny,

glistening coat but Irish words left
him with the most peculiar

smell, attracting the barks in par-
ticular of wolfhounds and red

setters, water spaniels, Kerry
Blues, and the keening of priests who

prayed only in hidden ditches
near forgotten limestone mass rocks.

The Fate of Dogs That Talk

He told The Washington Post *that he hears in house pets not just vowel qualities but intonation, syllabicity, rhythm "and, amazingly some consonantal strictures."*

The woman too poor to buy pigs' heads walks
home with dogs' heads, two sly-faced Samoyeds.

She's sure the ears, the eyes, the brain of each
will be so sapid. The roasted skin makes for good

tangy crackling – the fur will be a strain to shave.
All the while she will crave their tongues, framed

by sharp fangs, shamed now by finessing flies
scoffing like motes, in and out of the pearling throats.

When alive the dogs were mouthy mutts, run-offs
from a Romanian circus. Proud as Romanovs. All

the words they pronounced were perfect for the quays
of Tomis, but useless in the back alleys of Minsk.

No one there countenanced the mimicked pleas
of a Sorescu. Even 'mama' won no rescue from deaf ears,

mama the first moniker they mumbled as pups, while matching
wits at the dinner table, with the barely able family-baby

for spoons of mushy, soaked-with-gravy potato.
Their ring-side master still rues the day his cash-machine

canines absconded like deserting janissaries. He ponders
the mysteries of their whereabouts, unlike the woman too poor

for pigs' heads. Later she touts their toasted tongues:
"So flavoursome and delectable" so she can buy more dogs' heads.

At the Butcher's

The sheep's severed head seems merely disembodied;
floating, not hanging from a hook; eyes creamy and dozing
in a sheen of deep thought, as if she remembers the pastures,

the smell of shook clover, hedges to be jumped over,
the raptures of mad rams later dismembered. A stumped
man following his wife to the butcher's shop stares

into the sheep's lifeless eyes, his moist nose inches
from her muzzle; his puzzlement in gazing
not as if he would eat but befriend, as if social censure

is all that stops him from rending the sheep a kiss, stroking
her brow, missing an appreciative bahful greeting lopped
from the bodiless being. He turns in time to shirk his wife

who pays for lamb chops and piquant kidneys
with token pounds and broken smirks.

The Lee Road Codex

O'Sullivan

The man with the old Leica had just one subject:
left eyes – not right eyes, not whole faces;
left eyes blinking, left eyes winking

left eyes glaring, left eyes staring
left eyes squinting and peering, laughing
and crying. He photographed people eyes

dog eyes, cat eyes, cow eyes, sheep eyes
crow eyes. He bought a special
microscope lens-adapter and photographed

spider eyes – always the most lefty of the eight.
At first, he photographed whole faces
and cropped everything out except the left eye

but then he developed the confidence to focus
on the eye alone, from all angles, in all shades
of light, even in darkness, reflecting the moon.

When it came to the eyes of the dead
he had no access to battlefields or morgues
so he would steal into funeral homes, approach

a solitary corpse laid out in open casket, pin back
the eyelid and snap. Then he went to market
and captured the eyes of severed pork heads;

he swept along the fish stall snapping salmon
shark, tuna, mackerel, monk and plaice.
He processed and printed the negatives

on special luminous card, hung them on his ceiling,
so he would ease himself into sleep
staring at constellations of eyes, left ones.

Wrath Redux

for Matthew Sweeney

A hotel of turf is what he'd build.
The walls, the ceilings all formed
from peat still seeping as if with tea;

sodden bricks which would crisp
in the sun if packed and neatly stacked.
But his would remain fully filled with fluid

flowing from the living, breathing
bog beneath. All beds he'd weave
from still sprouting sphagnum

and windows dress with rushes black.
For breakfast, guests would feast
on vintage butter centuries old

– spread like chrism on best
soda bread – scooped from robust
baskets of blackened wicker

sunk in damp internment
for innumerable generations
where no living germ

could intrude. Chairs
would be chiselled
from millennia old oak,

and if the bronze-aged corpse
of a man ritually killed
should emerge with the butter

and the oak, he'd drink with it
the finest flavoured poteen
from water drawn near the body,

richer than any Hebridean spirit
priced as gold. And he'd sniff
the cadaver's crown coiffured

with pine lacquer hauled three thousand
years or more ago across the Pyrenees
to decorate a prehistoric playboy

before the cuckolds he'd made
unmade *him* with blows and cuts
as rhythmic as the scythes of work.

from 1001 Estonian Nights

i.m. Andres Ehin

One evening, as I travelled along the forest-fronted
road to Rapla, not too late, nineteen eighty-three
while summer simmered to its end with shortening

days and the sky was full of geese drifting by
in shaftless arrows, my attention lapsed on the almost
empty road built flat and wide for armoured columns

to lumber over. My little Trabant, blue and farting,
collided almost with a green man and his stricken
silver craft. I stopped to say sorry but he merely aimed

a gnarly finger at the slowly arriving stars pressing
their way through dusk's veil and asked for directions
in Estonian so impeccable, vowel lengths so exact,

his use of the abessive case so apt, no Western agent
could have mastered in a sun's lifetime; no American
with oxidised copper facepaint; no Brit with a beauty

mask of dried green tea; no misplaced Irish reveller
on March 18th. As the moments passed, and my
ignorance of Orion in relation to Cassiopeia

was obvious, I noticed his webbed feet and his utterances
change to honks of pain for his grounded state.
I've seen enough of men dying to know death is a taste

that visits them first on their tongue. His mouth frothed
with unimaginable heaviness in a dark, dark hole
through which the whole of his being was suddenly sucked,

machine and all as through a simple tear in fabric
which immediately afterwards self-mended.
I was left with just a breeze for company and the whiff

of stale lynx piss piddled by a queen in heat rising
from juniper bark at the forest's edge. I don't remember
how I got behind the wheel again, pressing on the accelerator

until the twin spires of Mary Magdalene's church loomed
into view, like the antennae of a Gothic spaceship.
I know I'm having trouble making you believe this.

Time Traveller

Now is before he was born. Days of air
shaken by bees, crow song probing eaves
and quays. Maker of the future a perfect
terracotta tense, a tense which sings.
The absence of push in his education
was presaged by the door's lack of wired
Sesame. He waits and waits for egress.
The door needs only his touch, its only
desire to swing. He waits for it to open
itself, as the cloud opens for the melting press
of the sun. He is ready to rot where he leans
leaving a breeze-blown blemish long after
he has arrived. Long before he comes into being.

The Discoveries of Thomas Fynch

Espenbaum dein Laub blickt weiß ins Dunkel
—Paul Celan

The talk of trees goes mostly unheard by man
but trees, like people, are full of feeling
and leaves are their vocal cords.

So discovered Thomas Fynch
who became aficionado of rustles,
expert on the Aspen leaf's sonic white poise;

who grew to know pine needles keened
before their boles were felled for coffins
and wrote of the chestnut's clack-clack

when slapped by raindrops and the crackling
of underground fire amidst the ash tree's rooted filigree.
He was born deaf, but his deafness was banished

when his infant body was passed by the village
healer through the cleft of a split juniper.
As the bush healed, the sound of the Earth

grew stronger in Thomas's ears. Among
his discoveries: the melancholy cry
of the Serengeti acacia is addressed solely

to giraffes who hear the leaves say "eat me, eat me"
in clickety giraffe tongue; undersea forests of kelp
record in analogue on their ululating thalli

the songs of extinct whales, replayed when caressed
by waters of a neap tide; graveyard yews draw up
through their roots the weeping of the dead

on All Souls' Day; the protests of gust-ruffled oak leaves
can be silenced at night by piercing the bark
with a beloved's toenails, clipped after a clamorous orgasm.

He plans to invent contraptions to help others to hear
what he and birds and insects hear, by combining
graphene nanowear with the ear nerves of bluebottle and finch

so even you can listen to the tulip summon the blackbird
when slugs attack or to the choral symphony
manuka blossoms sing to burrows of bumble bees.

Matador

The rain makes a prison of everywhere;
a million denizens in their apartment cells,
tram cars, taxis, staring out beyond
the beaded bars of misty windows.

Behind one glass pane is a white cockatoo
with a rainbow crest and a man who dresses
as a matador. He could be a matador.
He at least identifies as a matador

but his only sword is invisible and he spills
invisible blood, spring-like, from the jugulars
of invisible bulls, miniature bulls, not as small
as sheep or swine but smaller than the Irish

Moiled his father raised for beef, and more agile
with showy, bowy horns as pointed as a mother's tongue.
Often his bedroom floor is tidal with blood.
The neighbours would complain about the swells

of blood, sopping down their walls
on a rainy day; they would whine, whinge
were it not as invisible as it is unstenching
as the corpuscles wither and congeal

way after the silent noise of the clattering hooves
charging across their ceiling, and the silent booms
from the silent battering his walls endure during
the course of his battles. Nobody ever sees him

in his suit of lights with its sequins and threads
of gold and silver, yet it does saturate with sweat
and appears sometimes amidst the towels
and grey slacks, the white vests and blue shirts

surrendering to the wind on the rooftop
clothesline. He's convinced the cockatoo
in her cage hears and sees everything.
She squawks at all the right moments.

The View

A man hauled a window all day long, slung
     over his shoulder like a big wooden cross.
It was a sash window with nine panes.
      So many people thought he was a repairman
without a truck or some recycling freak
     on his way home from a dumpster. But really
he was homeless and liked to stare at the world
     through a window he could call his own.
He shook off the occasional offer of help:
     nobody else was going to get their hands
on his window. At certain street corners
     he would sit on the pavement and take in
the view between the little square frames.
      On the corner of South Mall he would admire
his favourite elm tree, the one with the bend
     to it caused by the wind; and on Sullivan's Quay
a big white and black mongrel who could be seen
     at the same time each day, strolling away
from Twomey's shop with fat wagging tail
     and a packet of *Tayto* clenched between slob
-bering lips. On Pope's Quay he placed the window
     on the curve-topped stone wall to watch
the swans floating by, heads rising and lowering
     on their curling necks. On MacCurtain Street
he watched the girls of Saint Angela's in their jade
     uniforms – the same his dead daughter once wore.
One day he stumbled, fell on his knees, then gashed
     his temple off the kerbside to save the glass.
One of the schoolgirls wiped the blood
     from his forehead with her handkerchief
while her classmates stood in a circle, swiping
     at the horrid scene through their phone screens.

The Town of Checkers

In the town where everyone dresses in black all the buildings
are white. Only swans and crows are allowed to alight.
All the food eaten is black or white. Sloes, olives, grapes.
Potatoes, bread, cheese. Bananas must split from their green

or yellow jackets at the town's breezy limits. *Citizen Kane*
and Woody Allen's *Manhattan* are everyone's favourite movies.
The pattern upon pattern of Disney's *Fantasia* would be
dismissed as mania in the town where only the end

and beginning of *The Wizard of Oz* are known. Nobody
has seen how Dorothy's shoes bled as they shone. When
the sky blurs blue they pray for clouds. Every home is heated
by a special oven which gobbles coal aloud while hiding all

flames deep in its black gusting brain. Snow is the most yearned-for
weather after black hail. Right at the start of life blonde and red-
        haired
babies are discarded in baskets on the outskirts of the next village
five rabies-riddled hills away. Chess is the most popular game.

Dice are played too but cards are burnt whenever diamonds or hearts
are thrown. The tarot is unknown so in three-year cycles a
        travelling nun
arrives and deciphers everyone's palm, dispels their fears, while for
        weeks
afterwards dreams are wheeling with colours no one has the
        language to explain.

Halloween

Black is to them as beige is to others.
From the house of the raging Satanists
the little girl dresses as a nun at Halloween –
full regalia: heavy wooden cross on globular
-beaded chain, severe distressed medieval wimple
like something handed down the generations
from Torquemada, swishing black habit, heavy
and simple as sin. She walks her street, eyes
turned often to the heavens as if witnessing
a hovering stalking angel, luminescent
with virtue, just over her head. She petrifies
the neighbourhood children by blessing them
and declaiming *et spiritus sancti*. Some would say
she is saving her own soul without knowing.

The Angel's Share

I

The child angel, a silver stream slithering from her left nostril,
is apprenticing as she stands by the dying man, enraptured
by her own sneakers glowing when she waves her foot.

Her juvenile wings, not yet sturdy enough to fly, shudder,
shedding quills. She is so young she hasn't yet had her talons
clipped for the first time, so her hands are covered

with rhinestoned white gloves. She sports bright yellow ribbons
in her hair like a Soviet kindergarten kid of yore.
Because she is still only an apprentice, she can do nothing

for the dying man. She cannot help his soul along.
And, over the hill, rush concerned, anguished humans,
anxious they cannot reach the stricken man soon enough.

To them the angel is invisible. To her they all comprise motley
elements of a boring scene. She awaits, with ennui, the return
of her celestial supervisor whose breath last stank

of distilled whiskey vapour.

II

Decades later, she's done the sex, done the drugs,
her skin is filigreed with unauthorised tattoos.
She is 'fallen' and can only rent herself out

to cheapskate undertakers to adorn graves and tombs
of people who cannot afford sculpted granite angels,
can only afford fleshy ones by the hour. Her best

customers hire her, anniversary after anniversary.
She prays when people die on sunny days.
Hoarfrost and rain distract her in her performance

and in cold and damp she curses the curses which extend
her penance, keep her stuck down here, ruing the day
her talons were clipped, her wings ever gave lift, empowered

her to make the choices which drew her away from above.

The Isle of Langette

for Mary Dalton

Yukon chinook were plentiful enough during river runs
for gangs of bears by every natural weir to fatten
on eating just the brains. They were known to hurl
the almost complete carcass into trees,
into the primeval forest whose hard green fruit
for millennia left an aftertaste of the coral flesh;
a taste I now caught lingering on my palate
as the ship I was sailing on aimed its sleek prow
at the largest river mouth of the lost island of tongue eaters.

Sources claimed the estuary was edged
by a well-fed wooden city, built from a forest
which always replenished itself with the speed
of sprouting nettles after yielding-up
pert parts of itself for fuel or shelter.

The tongue eaters were renowned
but rarely encountered; their island
veiled by a northern Sargasso of mist
and magnetic chaos. Only the lost
were said to reach there and for years
I tried to find myself lost
aiming the prow of the ship I sailed on
as if it were rudderless, the prow's
white sculpted spirit desperate to return
to the forest of its culling. I must admit,
near the end, I was sick of the journey
its interminable condition of never-arriving
like some pointless unspoken koan.

The tongue eaters professed no special wisdom
other than the wisdom of eating only tongues.
The world outside knew of this from the bottled missives
various in length, language, insight, vintage
which had re-entered the world their scriveners left
telling all of the elaborate cuisine of the tongue eaters;
their use of powdered owl tongue purely as a condiment,
how ox tongue and cod tongue were staples,
how lark tongue was flavoured tartly
with the sweetness of its own song and how
only the lost could find themselves there.
The bottles whetted my appetite for knowledge
and thus my culinary quest began.

Half-way through my search and desperate
I parted with the Nipponese gold I had made
from a thousand tuna for the white queenly prow
said to have been lumbered from the island's forest
– a forest full of lithesome trees
fed the tongueless corpses of a multitude
of beasts, winged, clawed, scaled, hirsute.
The bearded, prune-skinned huckster in St. John's
promised the prow was destined to return like a salmon
to the tree it was lopped from as an almost formless branch.
"Don't be surprised when it begins to yodel cat-like as it nears home.
It came from that part of the forest nourished by the carcasses of lynx."

Of course the world was full of tongues to be eaten;
the stewed and the deep-fried, the pickled and the marinated
but it was the secret of their preparation on that isle
which lured the likes of me. Until finally
slipping through the magnetic voile, the estuary,
the bright varicoloured city of painted wood
and the forest of unusual nourishment set the prow
to yodelling – something as genius as a Purcell fantasia.

Our unusual aria summoned a reception.
The tongue-eaters lined the quay-sides like needley teeth.
When I and the crew stepped ashore we were greeted
by speech which was a medley of growls and trills,
purrs and barks, shrill whistles and the howling of wolves.
The pitches of Mandarin, the clicked speech of savannah foragers
the excited screeches of chimpanzees were nothing to compare.
For days my crew enjoyed the company of the women
with their breasts triangular and nipples shaped like arrowheads.
The local men shared with me the seal-blubber flavoured liqueur
so important a part in ceremonies of circumcision.
Days and weeks passed and the rapture of lynx tongue
stuffed with shrew, fillet of *langue d'orca* marinated
in chestnut-fig and broth of braised rodent languettes
overwhelmed my wile and caution and I blurted
to the rapt inhabitants how I would tell the world
of the glory and detail of their recipes.

They scissored out my tongue and spooned it back to me
as a smoothened salve. "Consuming its goodness
will stop the stump from inflaming,"
they said in purring tones, in their own language
I came to understand after many, many years.

Coast Ghost

I plod towards the sea, a flaccid fish
swinging from my fist. The tide is low
and so too the beach gradient, so I walk
for ages, the waves furlongs away. I reek

of fish and though I can swim like a fish
the sea skips away from me, unzipping itself
from the land with a crude urgency, while sullen
bubbles of lugworms burp all around and crab

shells litter the crinkled foreshore like blown-out
hulks of miniature tanks. Kelp-wreathed limpets
mine stony outcrops acned with barnacles.
Shy anemones conceal their florid heads

deep in their necks. The fish I carry is dead.
My fingers bracelet its gills. I bought it
while its mouth still moved in silent supplication;
one among a mass flipping and glistening in the alien air.

What alignment of the moon yanked the current
which toted them into the trawler's nets?
I cradle the fish in my arms now, not spotted
like a trout or striped like a mackerel,

whether mullet or bass or something else
I do not know and still the waves retreat
though I am near enough now to hear
their white heads sizzle to a flat disappearance.

The Pebble Peddler

Last decade people scrummed
to purchase my painted pebbles
the acrylic-dipped, the gold-sprayed
the dabbed-with-brushes-
of-all-kinds-of-animal-hair

horse hair, dog hair, boar-snout hair
the hair of pygmy shrew
each imbuing the emotional
disposition of its origin
into the expression of the pebble

whatever the colour of the paint,
or texture of the stone:
lime, sand, bath or granite.
Some I shaped into globes
or ovoids, arrowheads or hearts.

The arrowheads were mostly failed
hearts which split after no matter
how much care or craft.
The point is, they were once
very popular at Christmas.

Though of no practical value
they sold to those who wished
to give them away, wrapped
in seasonal foil or dropped
in stockings. One woman told me

the arrowhead she bought
was for placing under the bedsheets
on her husband's side. A boy bought
a heart coloured blue, dabbed
with a brush made from a grey-haired

Rastafarian's discarded dreadlocks.
He posted it with stamps showing
Christmas angels with wings outspread
to a girl whom he had never even kissed
who lived on a sunny slope of the Tyrolean

alps – a blue which matched the lake there
and her eyes and the hue of his heart
since she had left for home.
But all that was last decade
before the crash, before malevolence

sorrowed everyone's pennies away,
sunk the weightless desires of everyone
you ever knew. My pebbles are not
weightless and my old spine protests
at their collective heft gathered

in my haversack which I haul
to my favourite pitch on a street-corner
where an old cinema and tearooms
have been remodelled into a dying
record store and fleeting fashion emporium.

The Art Deco embellishments I treasured
from childhood are concealed
behind plywood partitions and slogans
of commerce. I sell without desperation
since I need not do this for a living

and never charge more than shillings
meant to my grandfather, but still
people pass by with austere looks
and only the occasional will stop
look and touch, and fewer still

will buy with a mood, as if
they are doing me a favour, as if
I am a sad old man of little means
with nothing to offer but coloured stones.
They know nothing of the power

of my stones and I do not tell them.
I do not hawk. I do not squawk
out loud their qualities.
I merely sit quietly on my stool
of spalded birch and count

by the hour the dwindling custom
in these days of little hope.

ALSO BY PATRICK COTTER

POETRY
Perplexed Skin
Making Music

TRANSLATIONS
Moose Beetle Swallow: Poems of Andres Ehin (with Taavi Tatsi)
The Belling: Poems of László Lator (with Zsuzsa Kiss, Eugene
    O'Connell, Gregory O'Donoghue & Liz O'Donoghue)